WILD
EARTH
SCIENCE

T0009124

VOLCANIC ERUPTIONS

by Isaac Kerry

PEBBLE
a capstone imprint

Published by Pebble, an imprint of Capstone
1710 Roe Crest Drive, North Mankato, Minnesota 56003
capstonepub.com

Copyright © 2022 by Capstone. All rights reserved. No part of this publication may be reproduced in whole or in part, or stored in a retrieval system, or transmitted in any form or by any means, electronic, mechanical, photocopying, recording, or otherwise, without written permission of the publisher.

Library of Congress Cataloging-in-Publication Data
Names: Kerry, Isaac, author.
Title: Volcanic eruptions / Isaac Kerry.
Description: North Mankato, Minnesota : Pebble, [2022] | Series: Wild earth science | Includes bibliographical references and index. | Audience: Ages 5-8 | Audience: Grades K-1 |
Summary: "A rumble deep inside Earth. Hot, flowing magma is trapped and needs a way to escape. Pressure builds and causes a break in the surface. Eruption! Volcanic eruptions can shoot lava, ash, and smoke over a huge area. Why do they happen? Learn about volcanoes, what causes them, and how to be prepared"— Provided by publisher.
Identifiers: LCCN 2021042770 (print) | LCCN 2021042771 (ebook) |
   ISBN 9781663976970 (hardcover) | ISBN 9781666327472 (paperback) |
   ISBN 9781666327489 (pdf) | ISBN 9781666327502 (kindle edition)
Subjects: LCSH: Volcanic eruptions—Juvenile literature.
Classification: LCC QE521.3 .K46 2022 (print) | LCC QE521.3 (ebook) |
DDC 551.21—dc23
LC record available at https://lccn.loc.gov/2021042770
LC ebook record available at https://lccn.loc.gov/2021042771

Editorial Credits
Editor: Ericka Smith; Designer: Tracy Davies; Media Researcher: Svetlana Zhurkin; Production Specialist: Katy LaVigne

Image Credits
Bridgeman Images: © Archives Charmet, 23; Dreamstime: Martyn Unsworth, 12; Getty Images: andersen_oystein, 19, EyeEm/Yus Iran, 21; Shutterstock: Aeypix, 11 (back), Aldona Griskeviciene, 7, Asif Islam, 29, beboy, cover, 3, Dr Morley Read, 26, dynamic (map background), back cover and throughout, faridkei, 15, Gennady Teplitskiy, 5, Jack Ammit, 1, 4, JPacajoj, 16, Manamana, 8, MNStudio, 10 (back), pashabo, cover (logo), Rainer Lesniewski, 13, setyo adhi pamungkas, 27, Stan Jones, 9 (back), VectorMine, 9 (inset), 10 (inset), 11 (inset); USGS: 6, 17, 18, Austin Post, 25, Patricio Ramon, 20, R.G. McGimsey, 14

All internet sites appearing in back matter were available and accurate when this book was sent to press.

TABLE OF CONTENTS

Words in **bold** are in the glossary.

FIRE IN THE SKY

The earth shakes. Smoke streams into the sky. Hot **lava** rolls down the mountain. A volcano is erupting!

A volcano erupting in Russia

Volcanoes are powerful forces. Each year there are usually more than 50 volcanic **eruptions**. Most are small. That's good news. The biggest possible eruption could affect the whole planet!

WHAT IS A VOLCANO?

Volcanoes start far below Earth's surface. It is very hot there. Solid rock melts. It is called **magma**. Magma is lighter than solid rock. It rises up.

Vent

Lava

Magma

Sometimes magma rises through cracks. These cracks are called **vents**. Magma moves toward the surface. If it reaches the surface, it's called lava.

KINDS OF VOLCANOES

There are several kinds of volcanoes. They form in different ways. They have different shapes.

Cinder cone volcano

One kind is a cinder cone. It is made up of ash and rock. It looks like a hill. It has a large hole at the top.

Another kind is a shield volcano. Lava flows out of a vent. Then it rolls along the ground. The lava makes a **sloping** shape. These volcanoes can be miles wide.

Shield volcano

Composite volcano

A third kind is a composite volcano.
It forms when lava mixes with things
like ash and rocks. These volcanoes
go straight up. They create huge
mountains. Some can be 8,000 feet
(2,438 meters) high.

WHERE DO VOLCANOES FORM?

Volcanoes form all over the world. Scientists have found about 1,500 possible volcanoes. There are even more under the ocean.

Mount Erebus volcano in Antarctica

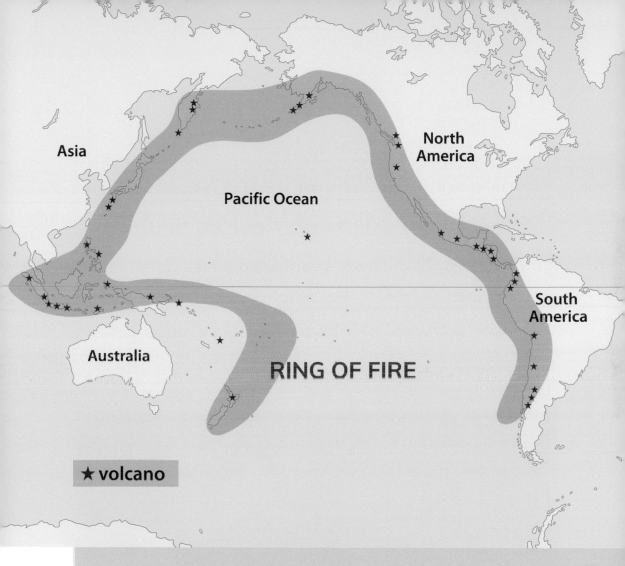

Asia

Pacific Ocean

North America

Australia

RING OF FIRE

South America

★ volcano

Some of the volcanoes along the Ring of Fire

Many volcanoes are in the Ring of Fire. This is an area in the Pacific Ocean. It has more than 450 volcanoes.

The United States has about 160 volcanoes that might be **active**. Many are in Alaska, Hawaii, California, and Oregon.

Indonesia and Japan also have a lot of active volcanoes.

A volcano in Alaska

A volcano in Indonesia

BOOM! A VOLCANO ERUPTS

There are two main kinds of eruptions. In one kind, lava comes out of the ground. It oozes down the volcano.

The second kind is an explosion. **Gases** build up underground. **Pressure** builds. It shoots out lava. The lava mixes with rocks and other materials.

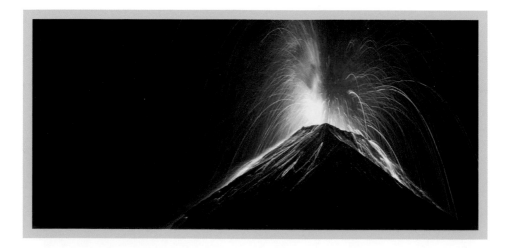

Lava flow from an eruption in Hawaii

Both kinds are dangerous. Lava is hot. It can be over 2,000 degrees Fahrenheit (1,093 degrees Celsius). It can burn buildings. It can block roads. This makes it hard to escape.

Volcanoes can make lots of lava. In 1950, Mauna Loa erupted in Hawaii. More than 492 million cubic yards (376 million cubic meters) of lava flowed from the volcano.

Lava flowing during the 1950 Mauna Loa eruption

Volcanoes can also produce a cloud-like mix of hot ash, gas, and rocks. This mix is more dangerous than lava. It can get as hot as 1,300°F (704°C). The clouds travel at speeds of 50 miles (80 kilometers) an hour or more. They are dangerous to people nearby.

Eruptions can also spread ash. Ash can travel hundreds of miles. It is harmful to breathe. It can also destroy crops and machines.

The top of Mount Tambora

Huge clouds of ash can change the world's climate. In 1815, Mount Tambora erupted in Indonesia. A huge amount of ash came from the volcano. This eruption lowered the world's temperature by about 5.4°F (3°C). This had a big effect. It caused crops to fail as far away as Europe.

FAMOUS ERUPTIONS

One of the most famous volcanic eruptions happened in what is now Italy. In 79 CE, Mount Vesuvius erupted. It had been **dormant** for hundreds of years. Ash buried the town of Pompeii. It killed more than 2,000 people.

The ash preserved the city. People have dug up the city's remains. They use the remains to understand Roman life.

As Mount Vesuvius erupted, clouds of ash fell on the nearby town of Pompeii.

In 1980, Mount St. Helens erupted in the state of Washington. The eruption started with an **earthquake**. The earthquake caused the top of the mountain to slide off. That created the largest **avalanche** in history.

The eruption released 520 million tons of ash. The ash landed as far as 930 miles (1,497 km) away.
The eruption killed 57 people.

STAYING SAFE

You can be prepared for a volcanic eruption. If you live close to a volcano, ask your family to make a plan to leave if needed.

Many communities have warning systems. They will let you know if an eruption is happening.

People protecting themselves from falling ash

If you have to leave, travel away from where the wind is blowing. You don't want to breathe in ash. Wear a mask if you must be outside while ash is falling.

BENEFITS OF VOLCANIC ERUPTIONS

Volcanoes are not all bad! Volcanic ash goes into the ground. It makes good soil. This soil is perfect for farming.

Underwater volcanic eruptions can create new islands. The Hawaiian Islands formed that way.

Our planet is warming. But ashes and gases from volcanoes can help cool the planet.

Kauai Island of Hawaii

GLOSSARY

active (ACK-tiv)—having a history of eruptions or likely to erupt

avalanche (A-vuh-lanch)—a mass of snow, rocks, ice, or soil that slides down a mountain slope

dormant (DOR-muhnt)—not active; dormant volcanoes have not erupted for a very long time

earthquake (ERTH-kwayk)—a sudden, violent shaking of the ground; earthquakes are caused by shifting of Earth's crust

eruption (ih-RUP-shuhn)—the action of sending out rock, hot ash, and lava from a volcano with great force

gas (GASS)—something that is not solid or liquid and does not have a definite shape

lava (LAH-vuh)—the hot, liquid rock that pours out of a volcano when it erupts

magma (MAG-muh)—melted rock found under the Earth's surface

pressure (PRESH-ur)—the force produced by pressing on something

sloping (SLOHP-ing)—slanted; having one end higher than the other

vent (VENT)—a hole in a volcano; hot ash, steam, and lava blow out of vents from an erupting volcano

READ MORE

Galat, Joan Marie. *Erupt!: 100 Fun Facts About Volcanoes*. Washington, D.C.: National Geographic Partners LLC, 2017.

Jacobs, Robin. *Earth-Shattering Events: Volcanoes, Earthquakes, Cyclones, Tsunamis and Other Natural Disasters*. London: Cicada Books, 2020.

Rose, Simon. *Amazing Volcanoes Around the World*. North Mankato, MN: Capstone, 2019.

INTERNET SITES

National Geographic Kids: "17 Explosive Volcano Facts!"
natgeokids.com/uk/discover/geography/physical-geography/volcano-facts

PlanBee: "Facts about Volcanoes for Children and Teachers"
planbee.com/blogs/news/facts-about-volcanoes-for-children-and-teachers

Weather Wiz Kidz: "Volcanoes"
weatherwizkids.com/weather-volcano.htm

INDEX

ABOUT THE AUTHOR

Isaac Kerry is an author, stay-at-home dad, and firefighter. He lives in Minnesota with his wife, two daughters, and an assortment of cats and dogs. When not engaged in writing, kid wrangling, or extinguishing fires, he loves reading, working out, and playing board games.